Easy Origami

John Montroll

Dover Publications, Inc., New York

Easy Origami is a new work, first published by Dover Publications, Inc., in 1992.

Library of Congress Cataloging-in-Publication Data

Montroll, John.
    Easy origami / John Montroll.
        p.   cm.
    ISBN-13: 978-0-486-27298-6 (pbk.)
    ISBN-10: 0-486-27298-2 (pbk.)
    1. Origami. I. Title.
TT870.M554 1992
736′.982—dc20

                                         92-16933
                                       CIP

Manufactured in the United States by Courier Corporation
27298220   2014
www.doverpublications.com

Introduction

I have compiled this collection of traditional Japanese projects for beginners in the hope of sparking a life-long interest in this ancient, elegant art. The models you will fold out of this book, such as a house that turns into a piano, a sailboat, assorted boxes, and other old favorites should provide a good foundation as you move on to more advanced paper folding.

The diagrams are drawn in the internationally approved Randlett–Yoshizawa style, which, you will find, is easy to follow once you have learned the basic folds. You can use any kind of square paper for these models, but the best results and most precise folding can be achieved using standard origami paper, which is colored on one side and white on the other. In these diagrams, the shading represents the colored side. Origami paper can be found in many hobby shops or purchased by mail from The Friends of The Origami Center of America, a non-profit organization of dedicated paperfolders. For more information about the Friends, send a self-addressed, business-size envelope with two first-class stamps to:

> The Friends of The Origami Center of America
> 15 West 77th St.
> New York, NY 10024–5192

Origami paper, and a catalog of other available craft books, can also be ordered from Dover Publications, Inc., at:

> Dover Publications, Inc.
> 31 East 2nd St.
> Mineola, NY 11501

Good Luck and Happy Folding!

John Montroll

Contents

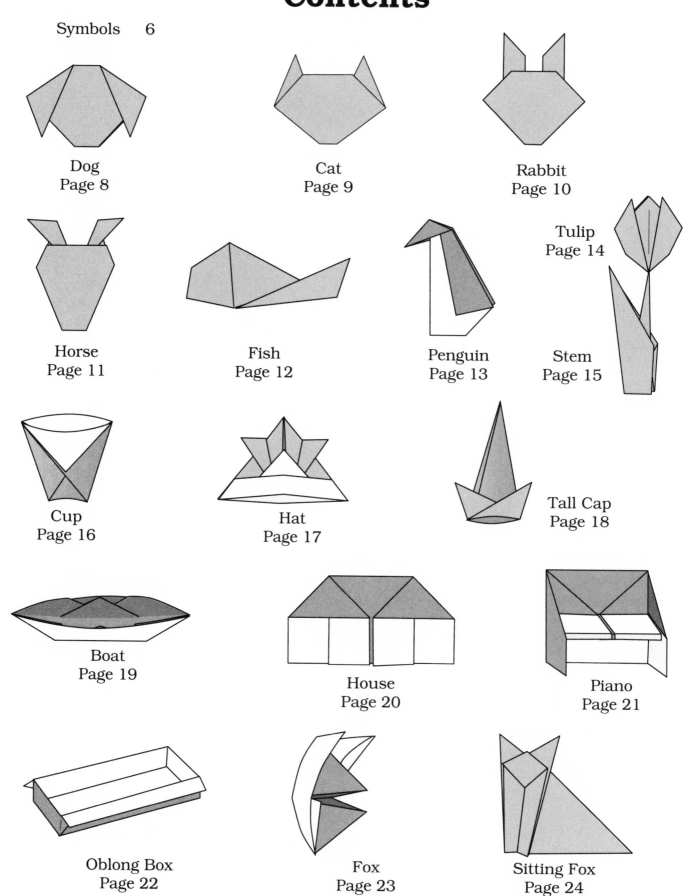

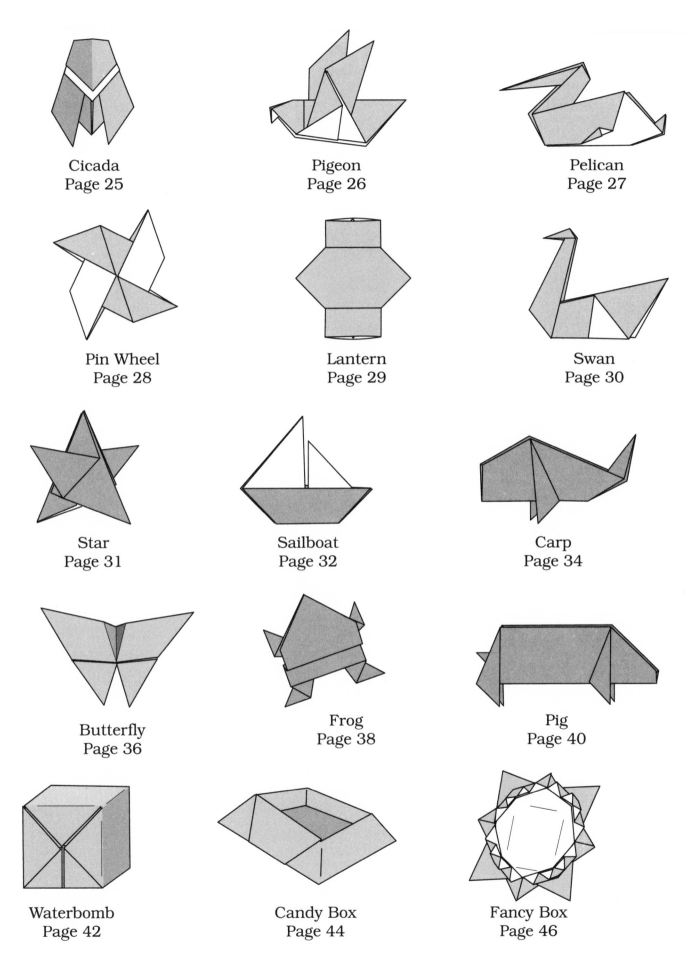

Symbols

Lines

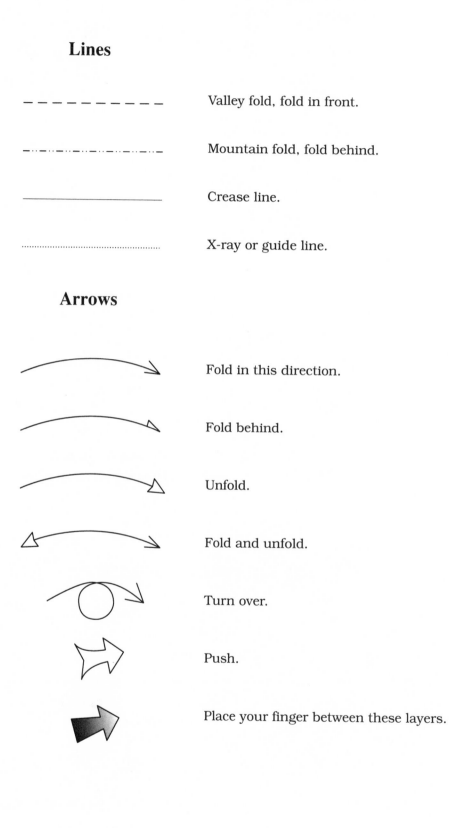

Valley fold, fold in front.

Mountain fold, fold behind.

Crease line.

X-ray or guide line.

Arrows

Fold in this direction.

Fold behind.

Unfold.

Fold and unfold.

Turn over.

Push.

Place your finger between these layers.

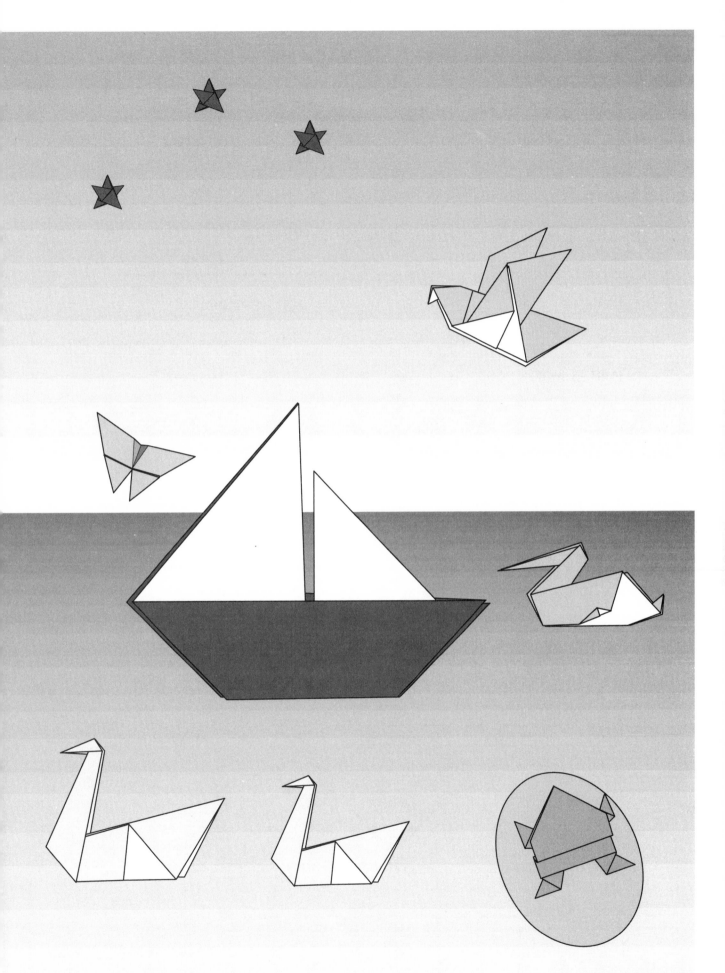

Dog

1

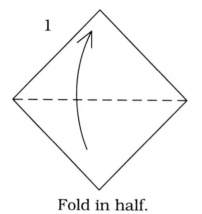

Fold in half.

2

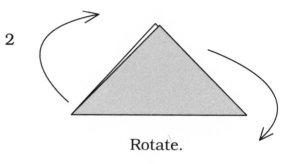

Rotate.

3

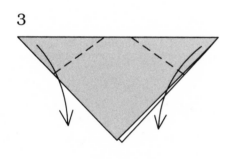

Fold the ears down.

4

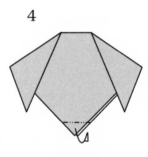

Fold behind.

5

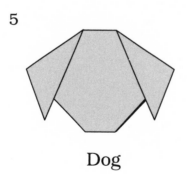

Dog

Cat

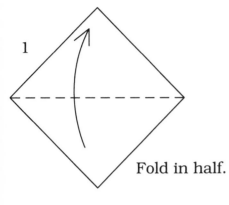

1

Fold in half.

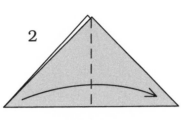

2

Fold in half.

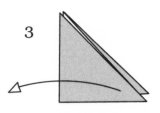

3

Unfold.

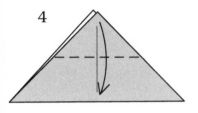

4

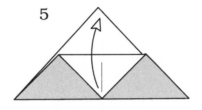

5

Unfold.

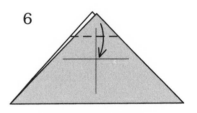

6

Fold both layers
to the line.

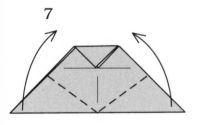

7

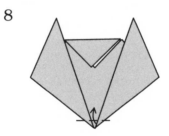

8

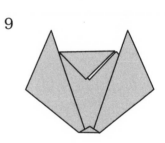

9

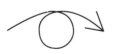

Turn over.

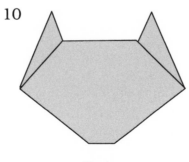

10

Cat

Rabbit

1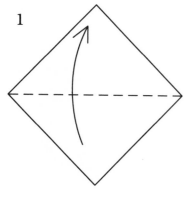

Fold in half.

2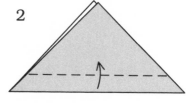

3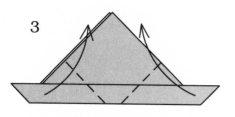

4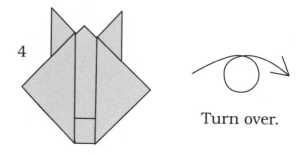

Turn over.

5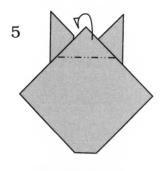

Fold behind.

6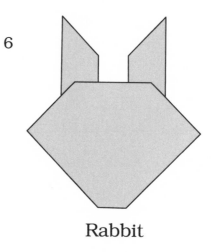

Rabbit

Horse

1

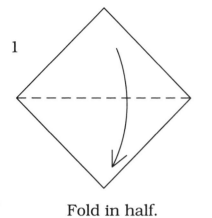

Fold in half.

2

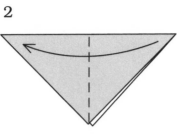

Fold in half.

3

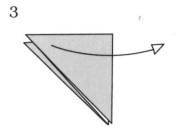

Unfold.

4

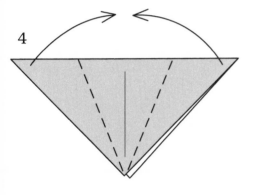

5

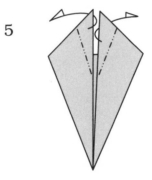

Fold the ears behind.

6

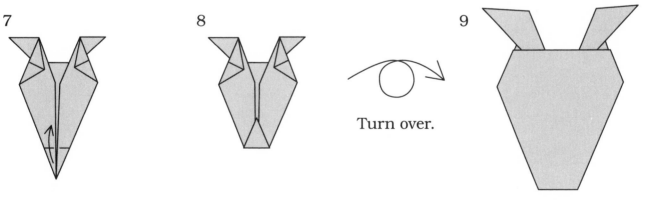

7

8

Turn over.

9

Horse

Fish

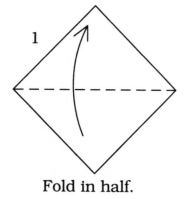

1

Fold in half.

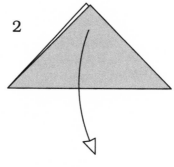

2

Unfold.

3

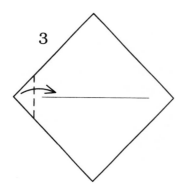

4

5

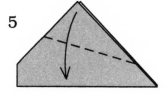

6

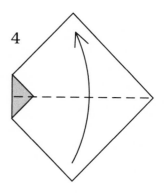

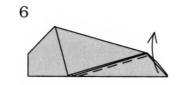

7

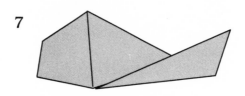

Fish

Penguin

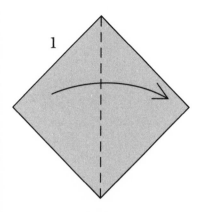

1

Fold in half.

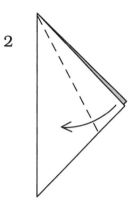

2

Repeat behind.

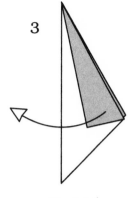

3

Unfold.

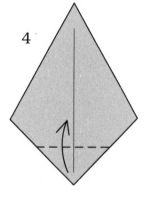

4

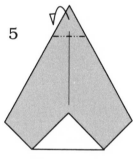

5

Fold behind.

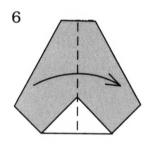

6

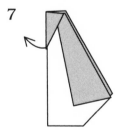

7

Slide up the head.

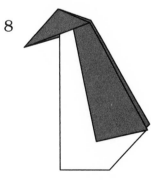

8

Penguin

Tulip

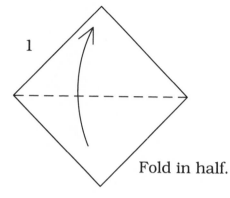

1

Fold in half.

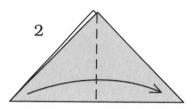

2

Fold in half.

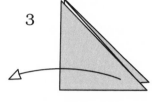

3

Unfold.

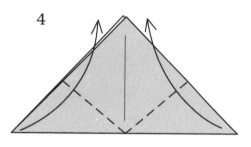

4

5

Fold behind.

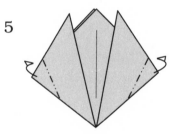

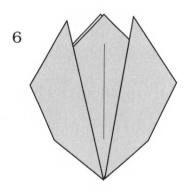

6

Tulip

Stem

1

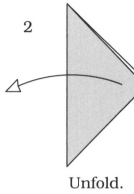

Fold in half.

2

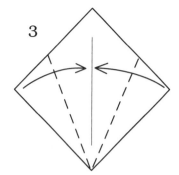

Unfold.

3

4

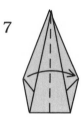

5

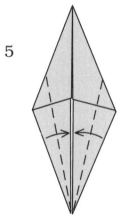

6

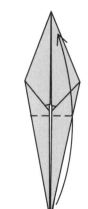

7

8

Slide out.

9

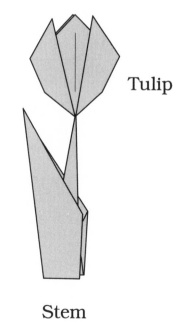

Tulip

Stem

Cup

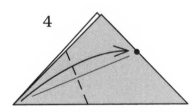

1

Fold in half.

2

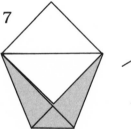

Fold one side down.

3

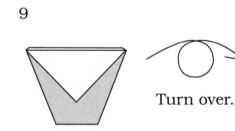

Unfold.

4

Fold the corner to the dot.

5

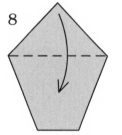

6

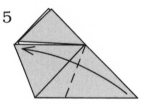

Fold one layer down.

7

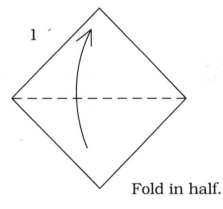

Turn over.

8

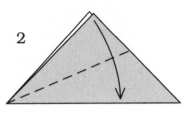

9

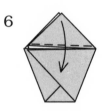

Turn over.

10

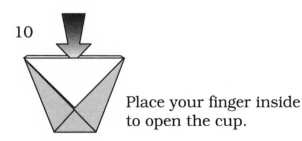

Place your finger inside to open the cup.

11

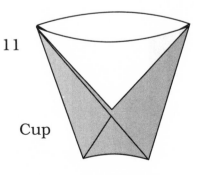

Cup

Hat

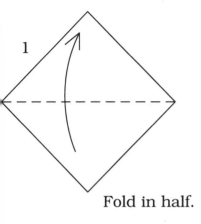

1

Fold in half.

2

Fold the corners up.

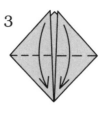

3

4

Rotate.

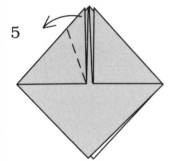

5

6

7

8

9

Turn over.

10

11

Turn over.

12

Place your
finger inside to
open the hat.

13

Hat

Tall Cap

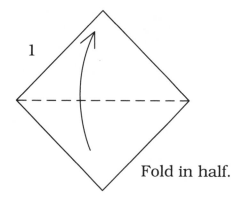

1

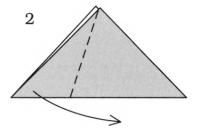

2

Fold in half.

3

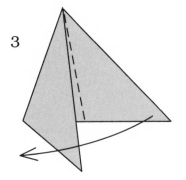

4

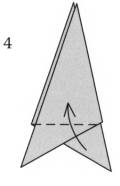

5

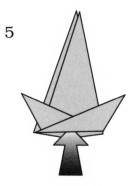

Place your finger inside.

6

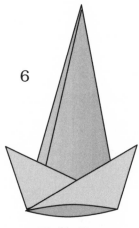

Tall Cap

Boat

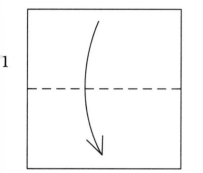

1 Fold in half.

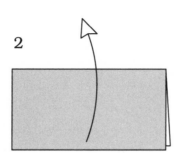

2 Unfold.

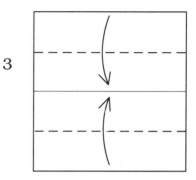

3 Fold to the center.

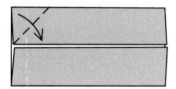

5 Fold a corner towards the center.

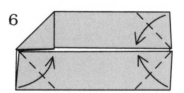

6 Fold the other corners towards the center.

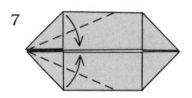

7

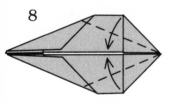

8

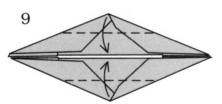

9 Fold to the center.

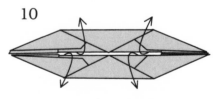

10 Open up to see the white paper.

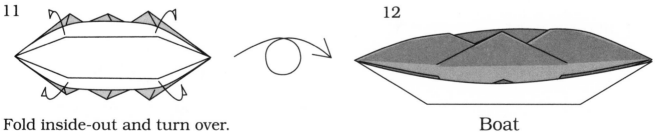

11 Fold inside-out and turn over.

12 Boat

House

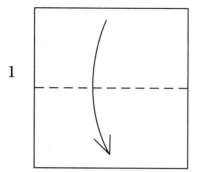

1 Fold in half.

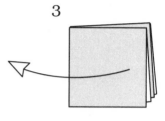

2 Fold in half.

3 Unfold.

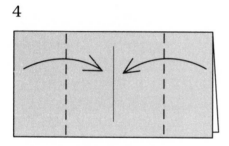

4 Fold to the center.

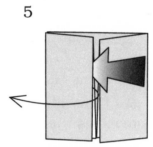

5 Place your finger inside to open.

6 Continue opening the model.

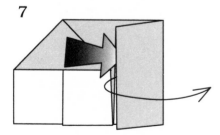

7 Open the right side.

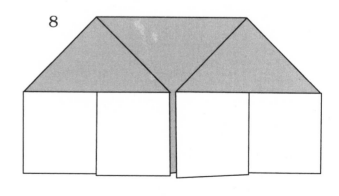

8

House

Piano

1

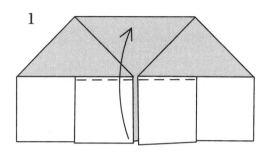

Begin with the house.

2

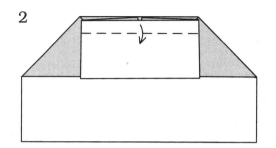

3

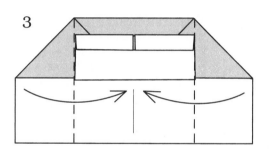

4

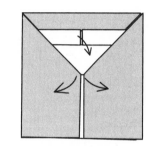

Open.

5

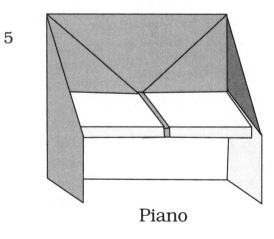

Piano

Oblong Box

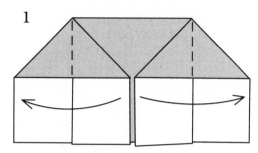

1

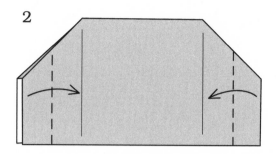

2

Begin with the house.

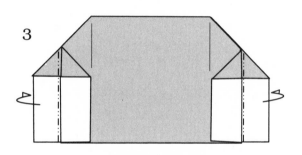

3

Fold behind.

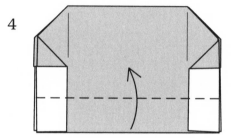

4

Repeat behind.

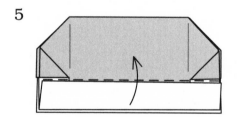

5

Repeat behind.

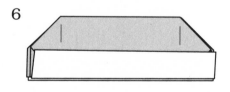

6

Rotate.

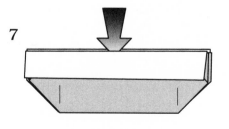

7

Open the box.

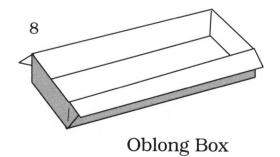

8

Oblong Box

Fox

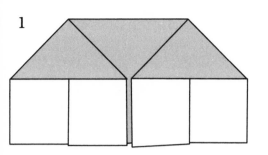

1

Begin with the house.

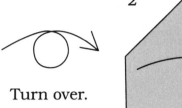

Turn over.

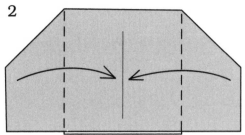

2

3

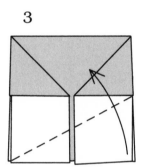

Fold up, repeat behind.

4

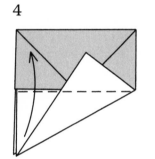

Fold up, repeat behind.

5

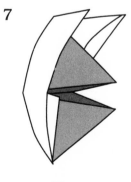

Rotate.

6

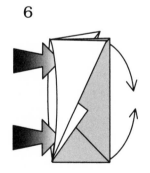

Place your finger and thumb
inside to shape the mouth.

7

Fox

Sitting Fox

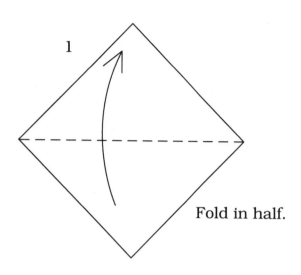

1

Fold in half.

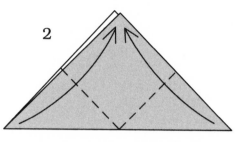

2

Fold the corners up.

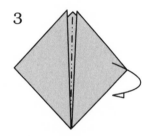

3

Fold behind.

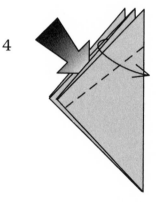

4

Open and rotate.

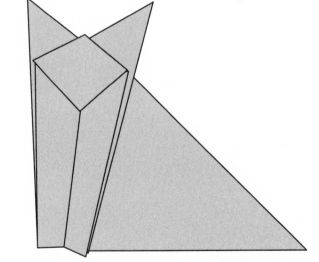

5

Sitting Fox

Cicada

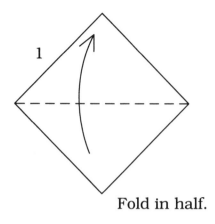

1

Fold in half.

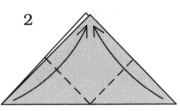

2

Fold the corners up.

3

4

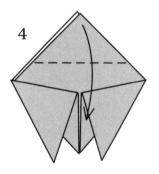

5

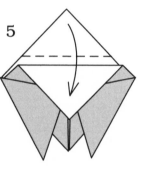

6

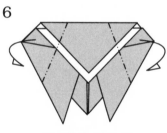

Fold behind.

7

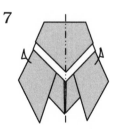

Bend in half.

8

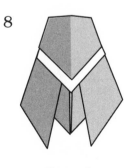

Cicada

Pigeon

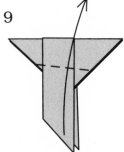

1 Fold in half.

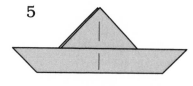

2 Fold in half.

3 Unfold.

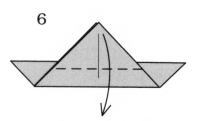

4

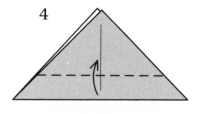

5

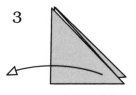

Turn over.

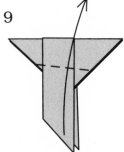

6 Fold one layer down.

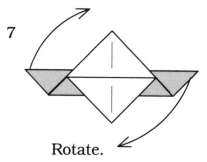

7 Rotate.

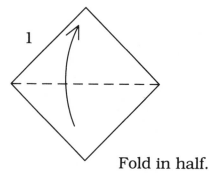

8 Fold in half.

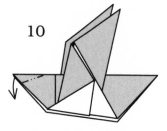

9 Fold the wing up, repeat behind.

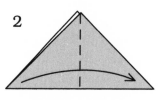

10 Fold the beak.

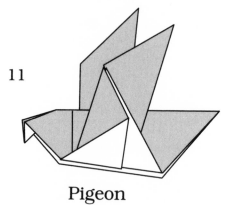

11 Pigeon

Pelican

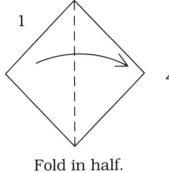

1

Fold in half.

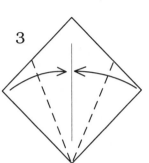

2

Unfold.

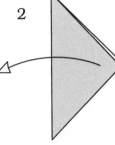

3

Fold to the center.

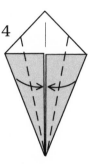

4

5

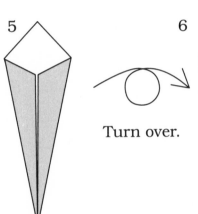

Turn over.

6

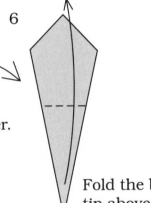

Fold the bottom
tip above the top.

7

8

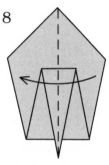

Fold in half
and rotate.

9

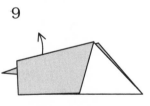

Slide out the
neck and head.

10

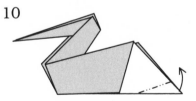

Fold the tail up.

11

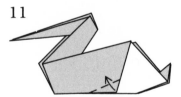

Repeat behind.

12

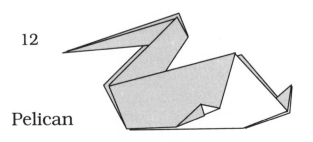

Pelican

Pin Wheel

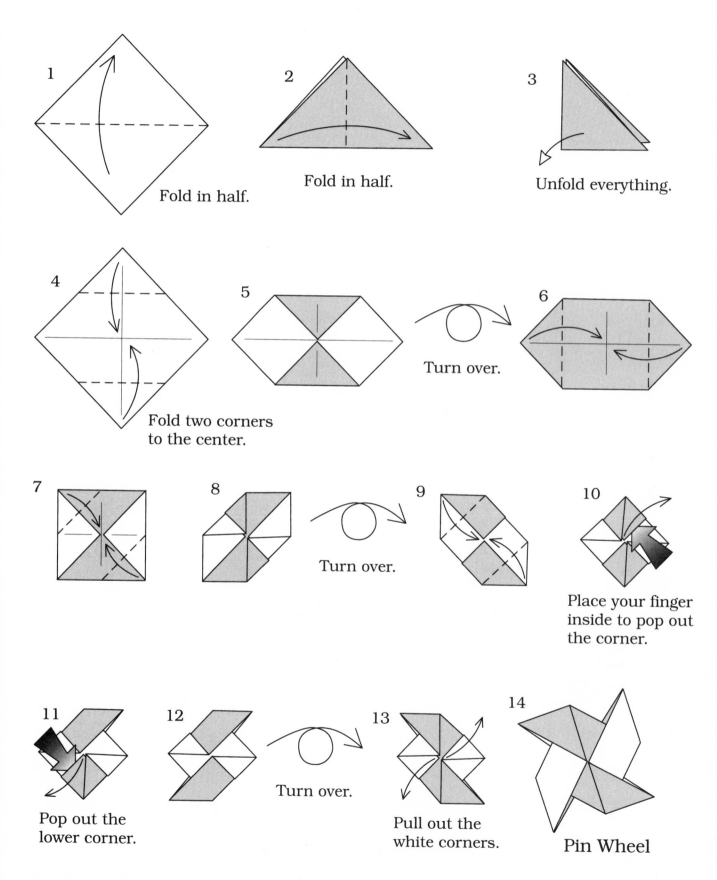

1 Fold in half.

2 Fold in half.

3 Unfold everything.

4 Fold two corners to the center.

5

Turn over.

6

7

8

Turn over.

9

10 Place your finger inside to pop out the corner.

11 Pop out the lower corner.

12

Turn over.

13 Pull out the white corners.

14 Pin Wheel

Lantern

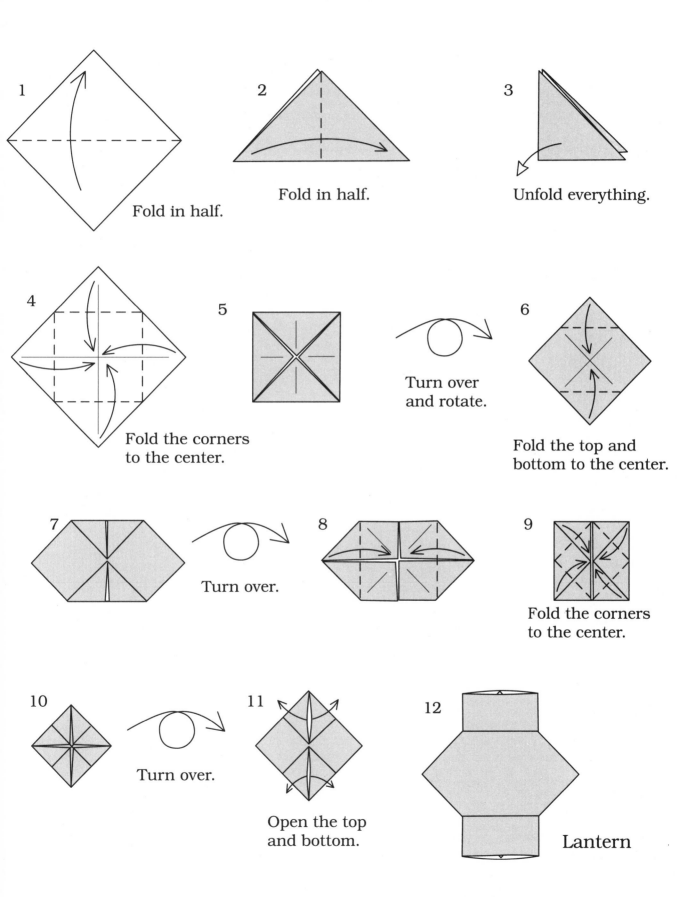

1 Fold in half.

2 Fold in half.

3 Unfold everything.

4 Fold the corners to the center.

5 Turn over and rotate.

6 Fold the top and bottom to the center.

7 Turn over.

8

9 Fold the corners to the center.

10 Turn over.

11 Open the top and bottom.

12 Lantern

Swan

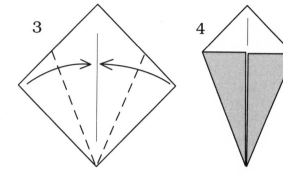

1

Fold in half.

2

Unfold.

3

4

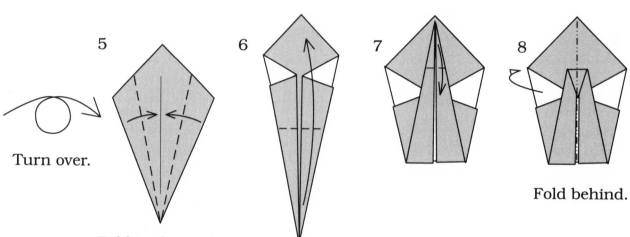

5

Turn over.

Fold to the center.

6

7

8

Fold behind.

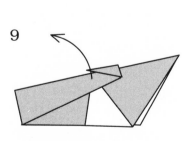

9

Slide the neck up.

10

Slide the head up.

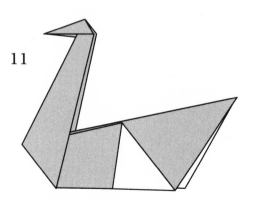

11

Swan

Star

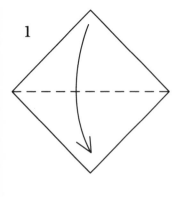

1

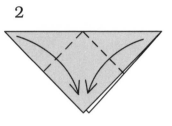

2

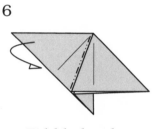

3

Unfold.

4

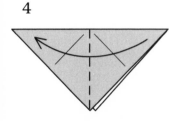

Fold in half.

5

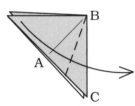

Fold A to the line B–C.

6

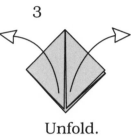

Fold behind.

7

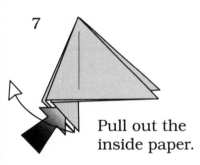

Pull out the inside paper.

8

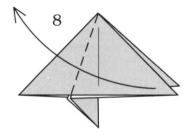

9

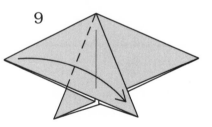

10

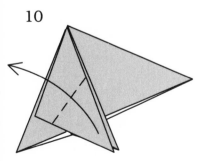

There are no guide lines for this fold.

11

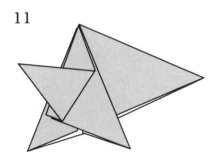

Repeat steps 9 and 10 behind.

12

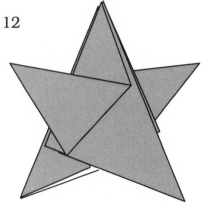

Star

Sailboat

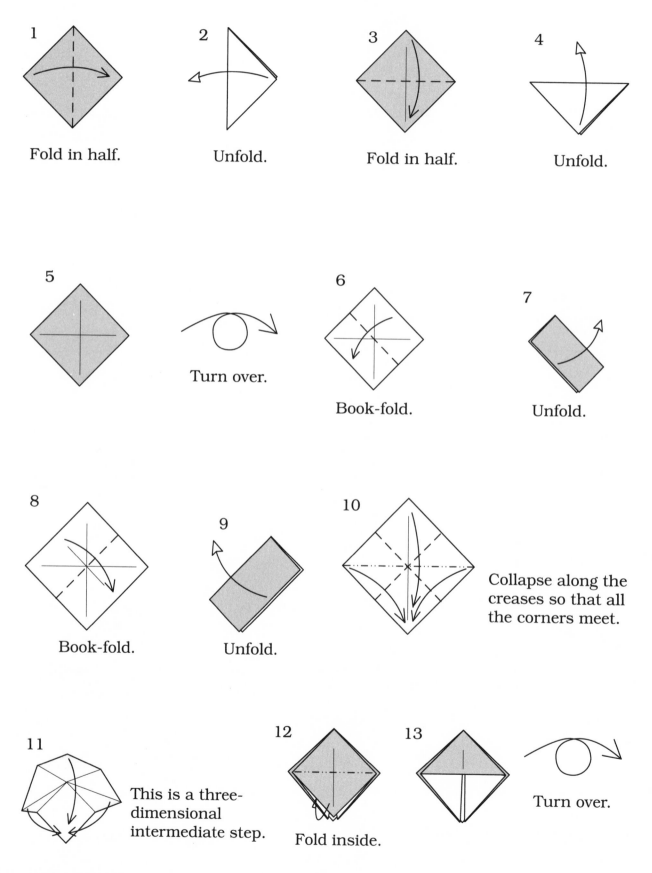

1. Fold in half.

2. Unfold.

3. Fold in half.

4. Unfold.

5.

Turn over.

6. Book-fold.

7. Unfold.

8. Book-fold.

9. Unfold.

10. Collapse along the creases so that all the corners meet.

11. This is a three-dimensional intermediate step.

12. Fold inside.

13.

Turn over.

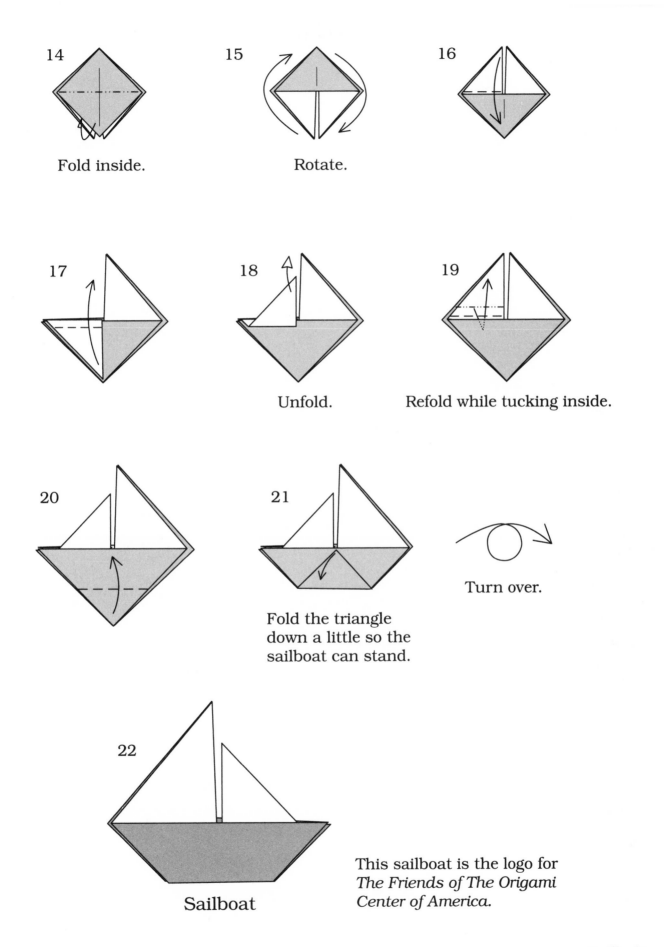

14 Fold inside.

15 Rotate.

16

17

18 Unfold.

19 Refold while tucking inside.

20

21 Fold the triangle down a little so the sailboat can stand.

Turn over.

22

Sailboat

This sailboat is the logo for *The Friends of The Origami Center of America.*

Carp

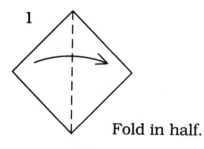

1 Fold in half.

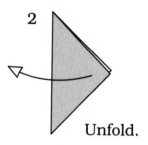

2 Unfold.

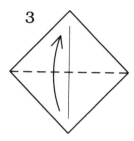

3

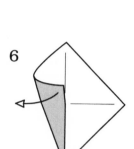

4 Unfold.

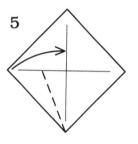

5 Kite-fold but only crease below the center line.

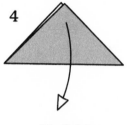

6 Unfold.

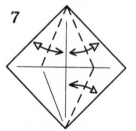

7 Fold and unfold three other sides.

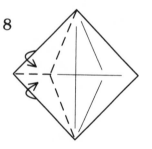

8

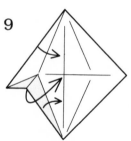

9 This is a three-dimensional drawing.

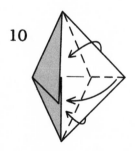

10 Repeat steps 8 and 9 on the right.

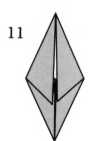

11 Turn over.

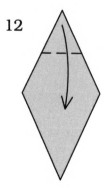

12

13

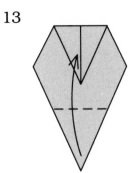

14

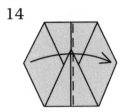

15

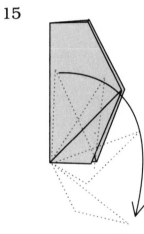

Slide out the point.

16

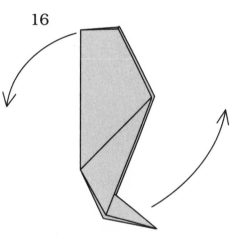

Rotate.

17

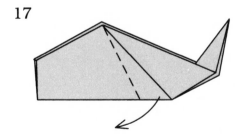

Fold the fin down, repeat behind.

18

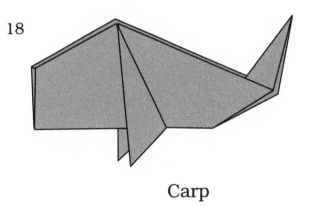

Carp

Butterfly

1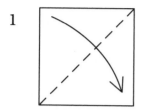

Fold in half.

2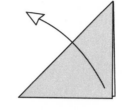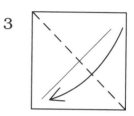

Unfold.

3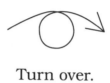

Fold in half.

4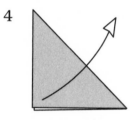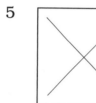

Unfold.

5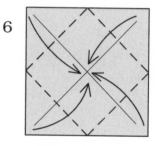

Turn over.

6

Fold the corners
to the center.

7

Unfold.

8

Turn over.

9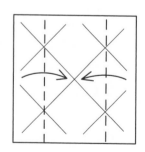

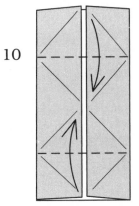

10

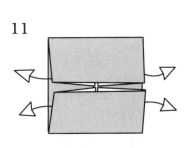

11

Pull out the corners.

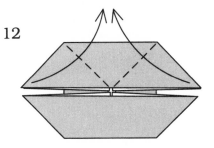

12

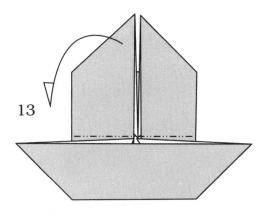

13

Fold behind.

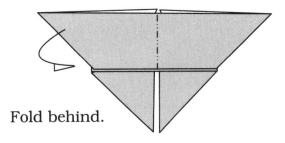

14

Fold behind.

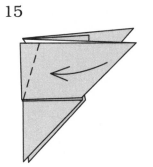

15

Repeat behind.

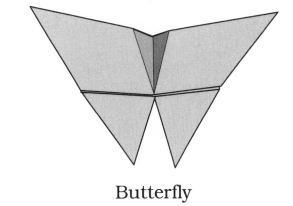

16

Butterfly

Frog

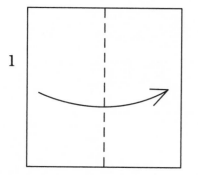

1

Fold in half.

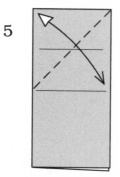

2

Fold in half.

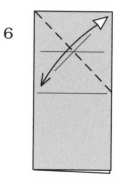

3

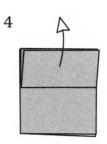

4

Unfold.

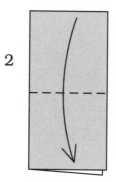

5

Fold and unfold.

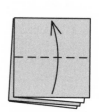

6

Fold and unfold.

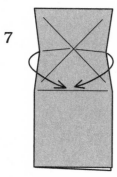

7

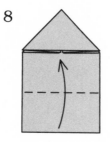

8

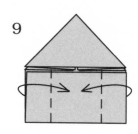

9

10

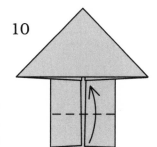

11

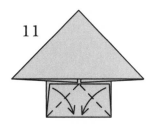

12

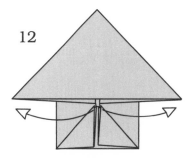

Pull out the corners.

13

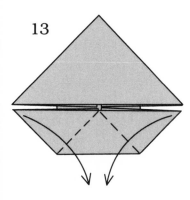

14

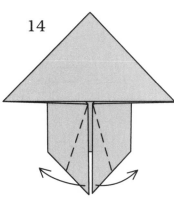

15

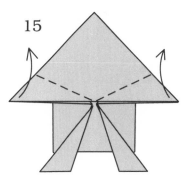

16

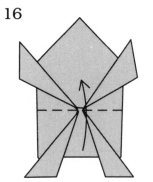

17

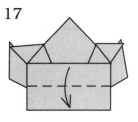

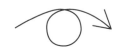

Turn over.

18

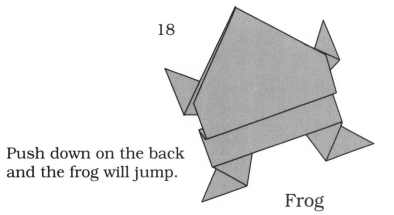

Push down on the back
and the frog will jump.

Frog

Pig

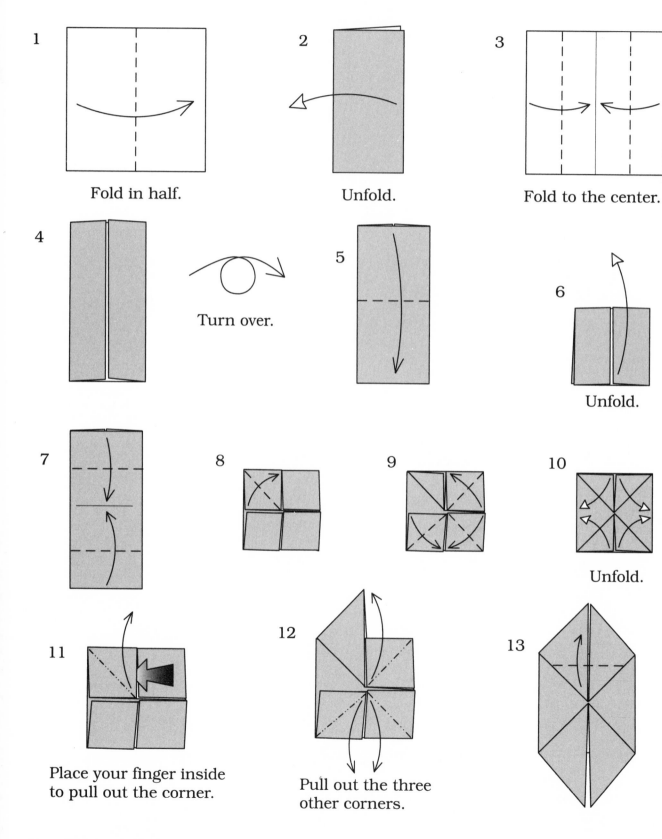

1 Fold in half.

2 Unfold.

3 Fold to the center.

4

Turn over.

5

6 Unfold.

7

8

9

10 Unfold.

11 Place your finger inside to pull out the corner.

12 Pull out the three other corners.

13

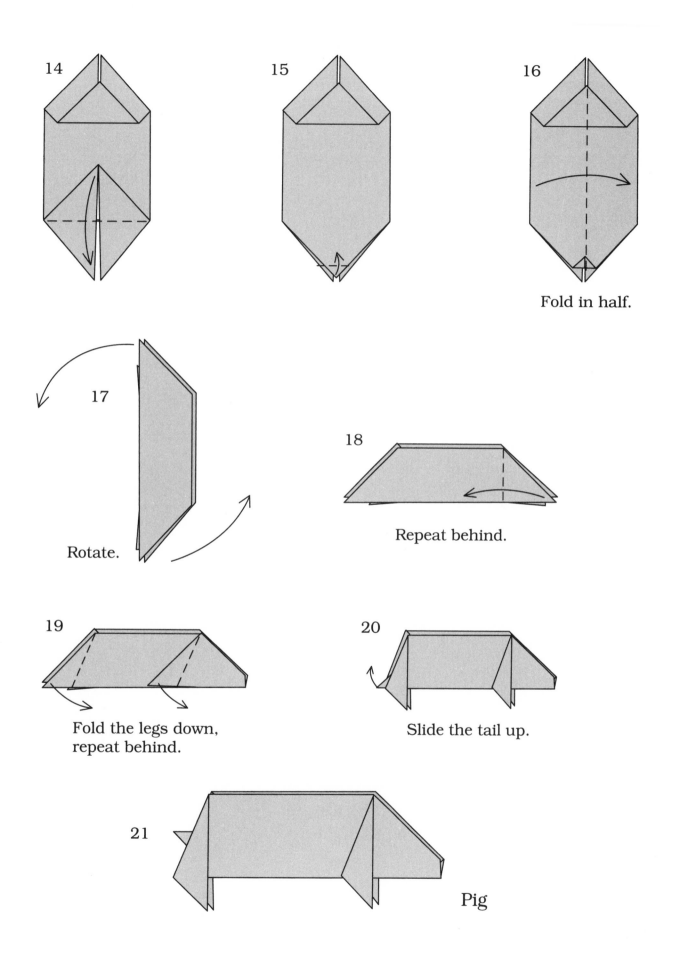

14

15

16

Fold in half.

17

Rotate.

18

Repeat behind.

19

Fold the legs down,
repeat behind.

20

Slide the tail up.

21

Pig

Pig 41

Waterbomb

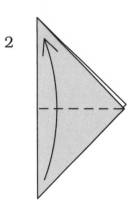

1

2

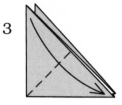

3

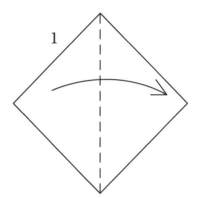

4

Fold behind.

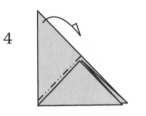

5

Pull out the middle layer.

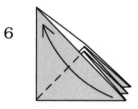

6

7

Rotate.

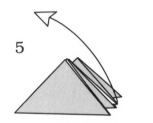

8

Fold the corners up,
repeat behind.

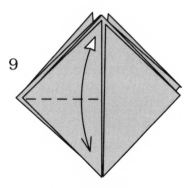

9

Fold one layer
down and unfold.

10

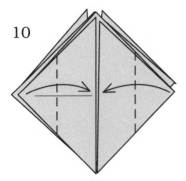

Fold to the center,
repeat behind.

11

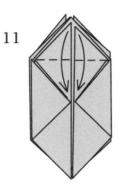

Fold to the center,
repeat behind.

12

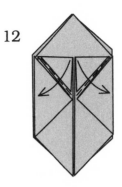

Repeat behind.

13

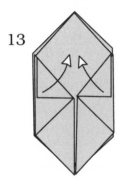

Unfold, repeat behind.

14

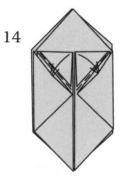

Tuck inside the pockets,
repeat behind.

15

Blow into the bottom.

16

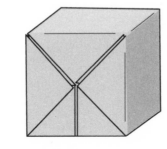

Waterbomb

Candy Box

1

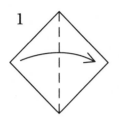

Fold in half.

2

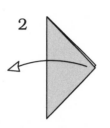

Unfold.

3

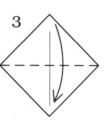

Fold in half.

4

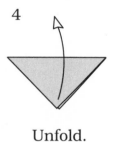

Unfold.

5

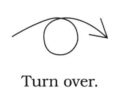

6

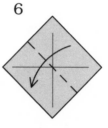

Book-fold.

7

Unfold.

Turn over.

8

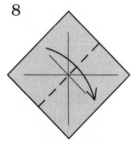

Book-fold.

9

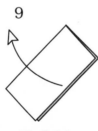

Unfold.

10

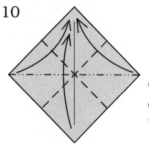

Collapse along the creases so that all the corners meet.

11

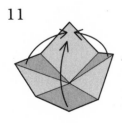

This is a three-dimensional intermediate step.

12

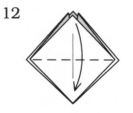

Repeat behind.

13

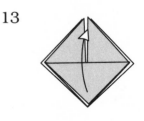

Unfold, repeat behind.

14

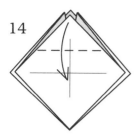

Repeat behind.

15

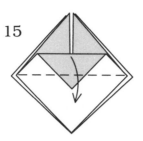

Repeat behind.

16

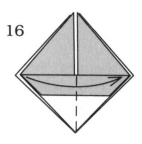

Repeat behind.

17

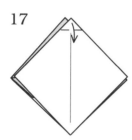

Fold the tip down,
repeat behind.

18

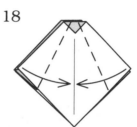

Kite-fold,
repeat behind.

19

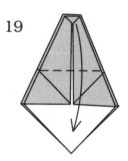

Repeat behind.

20

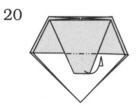

Tuck inside,
repeat behind.

21

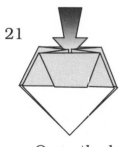

Open the box.

22

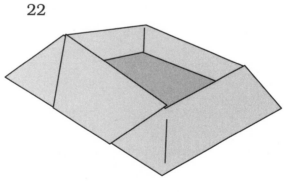

Candy Box

Fancy Box

1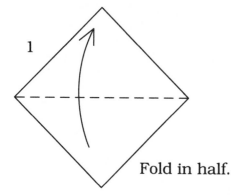

Fold in half.

2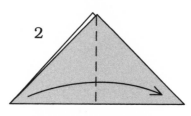

Fold in half.

3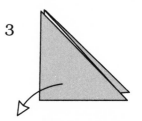

Unfold everything.

4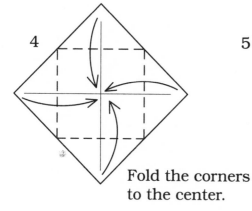

Fold the corners
to the center.

5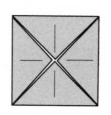

Turn over.

6

Fold the corners
to the center.

7

8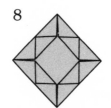

Turn over.

9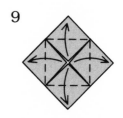

10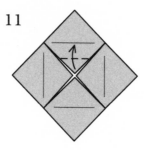

Unfold.

11

12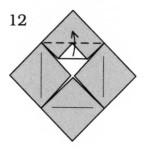

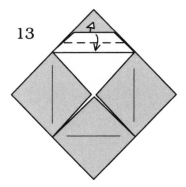

13

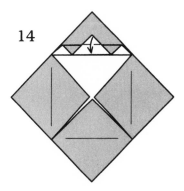

14

Let the corner slide out.

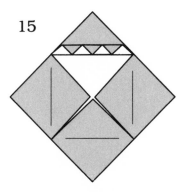

15

Repeat steps 11–14
on the three sides.

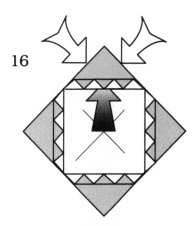

16

Place your finger inside and
push from the outside.
Repeat for each side.

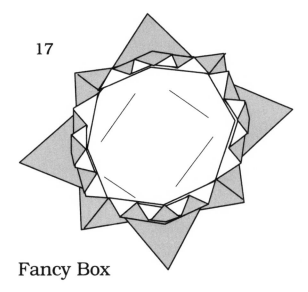

17

Fancy Box